Wishart

by Iain Gray

WRITING *to* REMEMBER

79 Main Street, Newtongrange,
Midlothian EH22 4NA
Tel: 0131 344 0414   Fax: 0845 075 6085
E-mail: info@lang-syne.co.uk
www.langsyneshop.co.uk

Design by Dorothy Meikle
Printed by Printwell Ltd
© Lang Syne Publishers Ltd 2022

All rights reserved. No part of this publication may be reproduced, stored or introduced into a retrieval system, or transmitted in any form or by any means (electronic, mechanical, photocopying, recording or otherwise) without the prior written permission of Lang Syne Publishers Ltd.

ISBN 978-1-85217-801-7

Wishart

MOTTO:
Mercy is my desire

CREST:
A demi-eagle with wings expanded

TERRITORY:
Kincardineshire

NAME variations include:
   Wishard
   Wischard
   Wisshart
   Wieheart
   Wisheart
   Wychart

Chapter one:

The origins of the clan system

by Rennie McOwan

The original Scottish clans of the Highlands and the great families of the Lowlands and Borders were gatherings of families, relatives, allies and neighbours for mutual protection against rivals or invaders.

Scotland experienced invasion from the Vikings, the Romans and English armies from the south. The Norman invasion of what is now England also had an influence on land-holding in Scotland. Some of these invaders stayed on and in time became 'Scottish'.

The word clan derives from the Gaelic language term 'clann', meaning children, and it was first used many centuries ago as communities were formed around tribal lands in glens and mountain fastnesses.

The format of clans changed over the centuries, but at its best the chief and his family held the land on behalf of all, like trustees, and the ordinary clansmen and women believed they had a blood relationship with the founder of their clan.

There were two way duties and obligations. An inadequate chief could be deposed and replaced by someone of greater ability.

Clan people had an immense pride in race. Their relationship with the chief was like adult children to a father and they had a real dignity.

The concept of clanship is very old and a more feudal notion of authority gradually crept in.

Pictland, for instance, was divided into seven principalities ruled by feudal leaders who were the strongest and most charismatic leaders of their particular groups.

By the sixth century the 'British' kingdoms of Strathclyde, Lothian and Celtic Dalriada (Argyll) had emerged and Scotland, as one nation, began to take shape in the time of King Kenneth MacAlpin.

Some chiefs claimed descent from ancient kings which may not have been accurate in every case.

By the twelfth and thirteenth centuries the clans and families were more strongly brought under the central control of Scottish monarchs.

Lands were awarded and administered more and more under royal favour, yet the power of the area clan chiefs was still very great.

The long wars to ensure Scotland's

independence against the expansionist ideas of English monarchs extended the influence of some clans and reduced the lands of others.

Those who supported Scotland's greatest king, Robert the Bruce, were awarded the territories of the families who had opposed his claim to the Scottish throne.

In the Scottish Borders country – the notorious Debatable Lands – the great families built up a ferocious reputation for providing warlike men accustomed to raiding into England and occasionally fighting one another.

Chiefs had the power to dispense justice and to confiscate lands and clan warfare produced a society where martial virtues – courage, hardiness, tenacity – were greatly admired.

Gradually the relationship between the clans and the Crown became strained as Scottish monarchs became more orientated to life in the Lowlands and, on occasion, towards England.

The Highland clans spoke a different language, Gaelic, whereas the language of Lowland Scotland and the court was Scots and in more modern times, English.

Highlanders dressed differently, had different

customs, and their wild mountain land sometimes seemed almost foreign to people living in the Lowlands.

It must be emphasised that Gaelic culture was very rich and story-telling, poetry, piping, the clarsach (harp) and other music all flourished and were greatly respected.

Highland culture was different from other parts of Scotland but it was not inferior or less sophisticated.

Central Government, whether in London or Edinburgh, sometimes saw the Gaelic clans as a challenge to their authority and some sent expeditions into the Highlands and west to crush the power of the Lords of the Isles.

Nevertheless, when the eighteenth century Jacobite Risings came along the cause of the Stuarts was mainly supported by Highland clans.

The word Jacobite comes from the Latin for James – Jacobus. The Jacobites wanted to restore the exiled Stuarts to the throne of Britain.

The monarchies of Scotland and England became one in 1603 when King James VI of Scotland (1st of England) gained the English throne after Queen Elizabeth died.

The Union of Parliaments of Scotland and England, the Treaty of Union, took place in 1707.

Some Highland clans, of course, and Lowland families opposed the Jacobites and supported the incoming Hanoverians.

After the Jacobite cause finally went down at Culloden in 1746 a kind of ethnic cleansing took place. The power of the chiefs was curtailed. Tartan and the pipes were banned in law.

Many emigrated, some because they wanted to, some because they were evicted by force. In addition, many Highlanders left for the cities of the south to seek work.

Many of the clan lands became home to sheep and deer shooting estates.

But the warlike traditions of the clans and the great Lowland and Border families lived on, with their descendants fighting bravely for freedom in two world wars.

Remember the men from whence you came, says the Gaelic proverb, and to that could be added the role of many heroic women.

The spirit of the clan, of having roots, whether Highland or Lowland, means much to thousands of people.

Meanwhile, many families proudly boast the heraldic device known as a Coat of Arms,.

The central motif of the Coat of Arms would originally have been what was sometimes borne on the shield of a warrior to distinguish himself from others on the battlefield.

Clan warfare produced a society where courage and tenacity were greatly admired

Chapter two:

The forgotten braveheart

Derived from the Anglo-Norman 'Wischard', a form of the Old French personal name 'Guiscard', the roots of 'Wishart' lie in the Old Norse *viskr*, descriptive of someone honoured as 'wise' and 'hardy' or 'brave'.

As we will find, this is a description which certainly proved apt in the case of one famous clerical bearer of the name who traced a descent from Anglo-Normans invited to settle in Scotland during the reign from 1124 to 1153 of King David I.

Having been temporarily exiled to the court of England's King Henry I, David had become enamoured of Norman customs and culture and, not least, their martial skills and organisational ability and, accordingly, found it to his benefit to have them as allies in his Scottish kingdom.

Tradition holds that one pre-eminent Anglo-Norman family who would come to take the Wishart surname first settled in Kincardineshire and, from there, other branches became established throughout Scotland.

A William Wishart enters the historical record in 1200 as receiving a grant from the Abbey of Cambuskenneth, in Stirling, to operate a mill while, in 1272, Adam Wishart is listed as being of the East Fife parish and village of Logie.

But one particular bearer of the name stands out for the pivotal role he played during the bitter and bloody Wars of Scottish Independence.

Described by the distinguished historian Professor G.W.S. Barrow as "indisputably one of the great figures in the struggle for Scottish independence" and as "an unheroic hero of the long war", Robert Wishart is nevertheless a forgotten 'braveheart'.

Of the Wisharts of Pittarrow, Kincardineshire, his date of birth is not known nor that of his relative – either a nephew or cousin – William Wishart, the former Chancellor of Scotland who died six years after being consecrated Bishop of St Andrews in 1273.

This was the same year in which Robert Wishart, having served as archdeacon at St Andrews, was appointed Bishop of Glasgow, subsequently proving himself as a staunch defender of the independence of the Scottish church and nation.

To find the root cause of the Wars of Independence in which Wishart was destined to play a pivotal role, we have to begin in 1290.

This was when, following the death of the young Margaret, Maid of Norway and heiress to King Alexander III of Scotland, John Balliol, son of an English nobleman, became a competitor for the crown.

There were several others, in what became known as the Great Cause, but Balliol's main rival was Robert Bruce, 5th Lord of Annandale and grandfather of the future King Robert the Bruce.

His claim came through the marriage in 1219 of Robert Bruce, 4th Lord of Annandale, to Isobel of Huntingdon, a daughter of Prince David of Scotland, of the Royal House of Dunkeld, 8th Earl of Huntingdon and whose paternal grandfather had been King David I.

Further strengthening the merits of his claim was that Isobel was also a niece of King William I, better known to posterity as William the Lion.

The Scottish nobility had – unwisely, with the benefit of hindsight – asked King Edward I of England to arbitrate in the matter of the succession.

Edward agreed but, insisting he be recognised as Lord Paramount of Scotland before giving his decision on the matter, he was reminded in no uncertain terms by Wishart that the kingdom was "not held in tribute or homage to anyone save God alone."

Wishart firmly sided with the Bruce claim, but Balliol was pronounced the rightful heir and duly inaugurated as such in November of 1292.

Despite Wishart's previous admonition to him, the ambitious and haughty Edward declared himself Lord Paramount of Scotland and Balliol was accordingly treated as a mere vassal, owing fealty to the English monarch.

Deeply rankled by this humiliating state of affairs, a number of Scottish nobles and leading ecclesiastical figures including Robert Wishart, David de Moravia, Bishop of Moray and William Lamberton, Bishop of St Andrews, concluded an alliance with France in July of 1295 – and Edward's response was to invade the northern kingdom.

As his forces wreaked fire and havoc, Balliol was forced to abdicate in July of the following year and, on Edward's orders, the proud arms of Scotland were formally torn from his tunic – giving him the nickname of 'Toom Tabard', or 'Empty Coat.'

Imprisoned for a time in the Tower of London, he was later allowed to retire to his French estates in Picardy, where he died in 1314.

The Scots rose in revolt against the imperialist designs of Edward in July of 1296 but, known as 'the Hammer of the Scots', he brought the entire nation under his subjugation little less than a month later.

Garrisoning strategic locations throughout the country, he demanded the signing of a humiliating treaty of fealty.

Subscribed to – reluctantly it has to be stressed – at Berwick by 1,500 Scottish earls, bishops and burgesses, the parchment is known as the *Ragman Roll* because of the profusion of ribbons that dangle from the seals of the signatories – among whom was Robert Wishart and the future King Robert the Bruce.

But subjugation under the iron fist of occupation did not sit well with the proud Scots, and the great patriot William Wallace raised the banner of revolt in May of 1297 – encouraged by Wishart and his fellow bishops who also wished to maintain the freedom and independence of their church.

A charismatic leader and an expert in the

tactics of guerrilla warfare, Wallace and his hardened band of freedom fighters set Scotland aflame – boosting the morale of their fellow countrymen as they inflicted a stunning series of defeats on the English garrisons.

This culminated in the liberation of nearly all of the nation following the battle of Stirling Bridge, on September 11, 1297.

But, defeated at the battle of Falkirk on July 22, 1298, after earlier being appointed Guardian of Scotland, Wallace was eventually betrayed and captured seven years later, and brutally executed in London as a 'traitor' on August 23, 1305.

His execution only served to further inflame Scottish passions, and the cause of the nation's freedom was taken up again, this time under the inspired leadership of Robert the Bruce, who had been enthroned as king at Scone in March of 1306 in a ceremony at which the three Scottish bishops including Wishart officiated.

Only a month, earlier, however, Bruce had incurred the wrath of the Comyns for the slaying in the Greyfriars Church in Dumfries of his bitter rival and fellow Guardian of Scotland John Comyn, known as the 'Red Comyn.'

The exact circumstances surrounding the killing remain a mystery, but tradition holds he and Bruce had become involved in a heated argument over the terms of a pact the pair are said to have made – culminating in the future king stabbing him before the high altar.

It was for the slaying of the Red Comyn, a deed that sent shockwaves throughout Europe, that Bruce was excommunicated by Pope Clement V – whereas Robert Wishart gave him absolution.

Firmly allied to Bruce's cause, Wishart even took personal charge of an assault on an English garrison at Cupar Castle, in Fife – ironically using timber the English had given him to help repair the bell tower at Glasgow Cathedral to construct siege engines.

Bruce was defeated at the battle of Methven on June 19, 1306 and forced into hiding, while Wishart was captured at Cupar.

Spared execution only through consideration for his clerical status, he was taken south in chains and incarcerated over the next eight years in a number of grim fortresses including Wisbech Castle, on the Isle of Ely.

Meanwhile Bruce managed to rally after his defeat at Methven and achieve a stunning series of victories over the occupying English forces that include the battle of Loudoun Hill, in Ayrshire, in May of 1307.

This latter engagement, featured in the 2018 historical action film *Outlaw King*, which has the Scottish actor Ron Donnachie in the role of Robert Wishart, was a particularly significant victory – using tactics successfully employed later in the decisive defeat of King Edward II at the battle of Bannockburn in 1314.

This was when a 20,000-strong English army was defeated by a Scots force less than half this strength.

As part of a prisoner exchange, the great warrior king Bruce ensured that one of the first Scots to be released was the loyal Robert Wishart who had done so much to help secure his nation's freedom.

By now totally blind and his body broken from his years of harsh confinement, he died in Glasgow in November of 1316 and was interred in the crypt of the city's cathedral.

Chapter three:

Keeping the faith

While in some respects Robert Wishart can be seen as a martyr to the causes of both his church and nation, in a later century one of his distant kinsfolk truly gained the unenviable distinction of martyrdom through defence of his faith.

This was during the seventeenth century period of religious upheaval the Scottish, or Protestant, Reformation that eventually led to a total break with the Roman Catholic Church and the foundation in 1560 of the Church of Scotland.

At issue had been fundamental differences in doctrine and interpretation of scripture between the Catholic Church and the 'Reformed' faith of those who 'protested' against it and were accordingly known as 'Protestants'.

It was into this maelstrom of theological dissension that George Wishart, of the Wisharts of Pittarrow, was destined to be immersed.

Born in about 1513, he studied at King's College, Aberdeen and the University of Leuven, graduating from the Belgian seat of learning in 1531 when aged only about eighteen.

It was while studying on the Continent that he studied the Reformed doctrines, incorporating them into his teaching of scripture when he returned to his native land.

In 1538, while teaching in Montrose, he came under investigation by the Bishop of Brechin on accusations of heresy and fled to England – where charges were brought against him in Bristol and he was compelled to recant what were termed his 'utterances'.

Believed to have visited Germany and Switzerland in either 1539 or 1540 – doubtless absorbing more Reformation doctrine, by 1542 he was back in England studying and teaching theology at Corpus Christi College, Cambridge.

Returned to Scotland by 1544, he gained fame as a highly charismatic preacher, travelling throughout the land to denounce what he perceived as the errors and abuses of the Catholic Church.

The dangers in which this placed him were so great that he required a personal bodyguard – none other than his loyal 'disciple' John Knox, later to gain fame in his own right as the 'father' of the Reformation.

But despite Knox's protection, Wishart was seized while preaching at Ormiston, Fife, in January of 1546 on the orders of the all-powerful Cardinal Beaton, Archbishop of St Andrews, Lord Chancellor and Cardinal Legate of Scotland.

Hauled off to St Andrews Castle and subjected to what was in effect a show trial, he refused to recant his Protestant beliefs and, condemned as a heretic, sentenced to execution.

On March 1, he was hanged from a gibbet and, taken down while still alive, burned at the stake – an added horror being that the cardinal had ordered packets of gunpowder to be sewn into his pockets.

But a savage retribution came just over two months later.

This was when William Kirkcaldy of Grange and Norman Leslie, Master of Rothes – whom Beaton had urged King James V to pursue as heretics – forced their way into the castle in St Andrews and murdered him.

Beaton's mutilated body was then hung from the very window from where he had gleefully watched the torments of George Wishart.

One of the many repercussions of the

Reformation, meanwhile, was that a number of abbeys and cathedrals were ransacked and 'idolatrous' images either defaced or destroyed.

Ironically, this includes the tomb in Glasgow Cathedral of the great patriot Robert Wishart.

Another staunch adherent of the faith was the Very Rev William Wishart, born in 1660 and later known as William Wishart (primus) and the son of the Rev William Wishart of Kinneil, Bo'ness.

The tumultuous seventeenth century into which he was born was periodically wracked by the War of the Three Kingdoms of Scotland, England and Ireland.

Also known as the British Civil Wars and of which the English Civil War formed a part, they were sparked off in Scotland during the Bishops' Wars of 1639 and 1640.

They had their origin in the widely unpopular attempt by King Charles I to impose uniform religious practice between the Church of England and the proudly independent Scottish Kirk, through the introduction into Scotland of the Episcopal Book of Common Prayer.

This acted as a catalyst for the signing on February 28, 1638 of the *National Covenant* – a document as important to Scottish history as the equally famed *Declaration of Arbroath* of 1320.

Described as 'the glorious marriage day of the kingdom with God', the Covenant renounced Roman Catholic belief, pledged to uphold the Presbyterian religion and called for free parliaments and assemblies.

First signed at Edinburgh's Greyfriars Kirk by nobles, barons, burgesses and ministers, it was subscribed to the following day by hundreds of common folk.

Copies were made and dispatched around the nation and supported by thousands more – with its adherents becoming known as Covenanters.

One of its later subscribers was William Wishart who, returning to Scotland in 1684 after studying at the University of Utrecht, was imprisoned for a time as a Covenanter.

Ordained in 1688 and minister of South Leith Parish Church and later the Tron Kirk, on Edinburgh's historic Royal Mile, he served as Moderator of the General Assembly of the Church of Scotland on no fewer than five occasions between 1706 and 1728.

Also principal of the University of Edinburgh from 1716 until a year before his death in 1729, one of his sons, known as the Very Rev William Wishart (secundus), born in 1691, also served as moderator of the church and as a principal of the university.

He died in 1753 while his younger brother the Very Rev Dr George Wishart, born in 1703 and who died in 1785, kept up what had become a family tradition by serving as moderator in 1748.

From the pulpit to the high seas, Sir James Wishart, a brother of William Wishart (primus), was the Royal Navy admiral born in 1659.

Distinguishing himself in a number of naval engagements against the French during the early eighteenth century War of the Spanish Succession including the battles of Cadiz and Vigo Bay in 1702 and, two years later, the capture of Gibraltar, he died in 1723.

Nearly two centuries later, in 1920, the Royal Navy destroyer HMS *Wishart* (D67) and which saw action throughout the Second World War, was named in his honour.

One of its commanding officers for a time was Lord Louis Mountbatten who, when trying to inspire his crew, is said to have joked the vessel had the best name in the navy – making the pun "Our Father Wishart in Heaven".

From the high seas to the contemporary worlds of music and politics, Peter Wishart, better known as Pete Wishart, is the Scottish National Party (SNP) politician and keyboard player born in Dunfermline in 1962.

As a musician, he played for the Celtic folk/rock bands Big Country and Runrig – performing on albums by the latter including the 1987 *The Cutter and the Clan* and, from 2011, *The Stamping Ground*.

Elected as MP (Member of Parliament) for Perth and North Perthshire in 2005, having previously served from 2001 to 2005 as the member for North Tayside, posts he has held include the SNP's Westminster spokesperson for the constitution and also for culture and sport.

Chapter four:
On the world stage

Bearers of the Wishart name have gained international recognition through a diverse range of endeavours and pursuits, not least as pioneers in the field of medicine.

Born in 1781 near Kirkliston, West Lothian **John Henry Wishart** was the surgeon who, practising as an ophthalmologist, founded Scotland's first hospital dedicated to the treatment of eye diseases.

Aged only 16 when he enrolled as a student at the University of Edinburgh, he later served a surgical apprenticeship and, in 1805, qualified as a Fellow of the Royal College of Surgeons of Edinburgh on the strength of an essay he submitted entitled *Ophthalmia*.

In this ground-breaking work, he gave an account of the conditions that cause eye inflammations such as conjunctivitis and how cases had increased partly as a result of trachoma that had found its way into the British population through soldiers returning from Spain and Egypt during the Napoleonic Wars.

Setting up a surgery in Edinburgh, he also contributed greatly to a wider understanding of eye disease by translating into English two important works by his near-contemporary the Italian surgeon and anatomist Antonio Scarpa.

In 1822, along with his former surgical apprentice John Argyll Robertson, he founded the Edinburgh Eye Dispensary in the city's Lawnmarket – Scotland's first such specialist hospital and which became a model for others throughout the United Kingdom.

Elected president of the Royal College of Surgeons of Edinburgh in 1820 and, a year later, made a Fellow of the Royal Society of Edinburgh, he died in 1834 while he lends his name to the form of cerebral tumour known as 'the Wishart phenotype'.

On North American shores, **John Wishart** was the leading mid-eighteenth to early nineteenth century Canadian surgeon and medical educator born in 1850 in Guelph, Ontario.

His lecture notes from his time at the University of Western Ontario are consulted to this day while, performing an appendectomy in 1886, he became one of the earliest practitioners of the surgical technique.

A founding Fellow of the American College of Surgeons and first surgeon-in-chief at St Joseph's Hospital in London, Ontario, he died in 1926.

Back on British shores and in contemporary times, **Professor Gordon C. Wishart** is the Scottish surgeon noted as a pioneer in the study and treatment of breast cancer.

Born in Edinburgh in 1960 and having studied medicine in the city, as consultative breast and endocrine surgeon at Addenbrooke's Hospital, Cambridge, his many award-winning papers on breast cancer have led to a number of innovative techniques, including infrared imaging, being put into practice.

From medicine to mathematics, **John Wishart** was the Scottish mathematician and statistician born in Perth in 1898.

Appointed reader in statistics at the University of Cambridge in 1931 and where, 22 years later, he became the first director of the Statistical Laboratory, his model 'the Wishart distribution' is so-named in his honour.

Elected a Fellow of the American Statistical Association, he drowned in 1956 after suffering a stroke while swimming in the sea at Revolcadero

Beach, Acapulco – having been in Mexico at the time to help set up a research centre.

Returning to a medical theme, but this time in the worlds of contemporary writing and film, **Adam Wishart** is the award-winning British author and director whose book *One in Three: A Son's Journey into the History and Science of Cancer*, was nominated for the 2007 Royal Society Book Award.

Born in 1969, his BBC documentary *Monkeys, Rats and Me: Animal Testing* won the 2007 Grierson Award for Best Science Documentary, while *The Price of Life*, examining the rationing of high-cost cancer drugs, won the 2009 award.

From documentaries to music, **Bridget Wishart**, born in Plymouth in 1962, is the English singer, musician and performance artist who sang lead vocals for the 'space rock' band Hawkwind between 1989 and 1991.

The only woman to have performed the role with the band since it was first formed in 1969 and featuring on its best-selling albums *Space Bandits* and *Palace Springs*, since 2007 she has performed with the band Spirits Burning.

In a different musical genre, **Trevor Wishart**, born in Leeds in 1946, is the English composer instrumental in the design and application of software tools for the creation of digital music.

These, for what he has dubbed 'sonic art', include the Desktop Composers Project while, from 2010 to 2011, he served as composer-in-residence at the University of Oxford's faculty of music.

Bearers of the Wishart name have also excelled in the highly competitive world of sport.

Named in 2005 one of the 25 greatest ever New South Wales rugby league team players, **Rod Wishart** is the Australian former goal-kicking winger born in 1968 in Gerringong.

Having made 22 appearances for New South Wales between 1990 and 1998 and played for his nation during the 1992 Great Britain Lions tour of Australia and New Zealand, he also appears in the 2006 film *Footy Legends*.

From rugby to the fields of European football, **Fraser Wishart**, born in 1965 in Johnstone, Renfrewshire is the Scottish former defender who played for clubs including Motherwell – where he made more than 150 appearances between 1983 and 1989 – St Mirren, Falkirk, Rangers and Airdrieonians.

Chief executive at the time of writing of the

Professional Footballers' Association Scotland, he is also a media commentator on the game.

From football to cricket, **Craig Wishart**, born in Zimbabwe in 1974, is the former player who made his Test debut in 1995 and who, at the 2003 Cricket World Cup achieved a one-day record batting score of 172 not out against Namibia.

From sport to the world of publishing **Ernest Wishart**, born in 1902, was the co-founder in 1936 of Lawrence and Wishart, for many years associated with the Communist Party of Great Britain.

Formed through the merger of the left-wing publishing enterprise Wishart Ltd. with Martin Lawrence, then the publication arm in Britain of the Communist Party, Lawrence and Wishart specialised in a range of works.

These include classics on Marxism, working class history, political economics, poetry, drama and literature, while ventures today include the journals *Renewal* and *Anarchist Studies*.

Ernest Wishart died in 1987 while, through his marriage to Lorna Cecilia Garman, born in 1911 and a member of the bohemian 'Bloomsbury set' in London, he was the father of the English figurative painter **Michael Wishart**.

Born in 1928, spending most of his career in France, America and North Africa and a friend of the artists Lucien Freud and Francis Bacon, his 1977 memoir *High Diver* caused a scandal because of his description of his hedonistic lifestyle.

Married for a time to the artist Anne Dunn, he died in 1996.

On Australian shores, **Felicity Wishart**, nicknamed "Flic", was the feisty Australian conservationist and environmentalist born to parents of Scottish descent in Melbourne in 1965.

Arrested and imprisoned for a number of days when aged 17 following an occupation protest against the impact of the Franklin Dam, in Tasmania, she went on to study environmental science and joined the Australian Conservation Foundation.

While with the foundation, she was instrumental in having the Queensland tropical rain forests listed as World Heritage Sites while, serving between 2000 and 2004 as director of the Queensland Conservation Council, she led a number of campaigns against land clearance.

Before her death in 2015, aged only 50, one of her last projects had been to highlight environmental threats to the Great Barrier Reef and, in 2017, the

Great Barrier Reef Marine Park Authority named a reef northeast of Hinchinbrook Island 'Felicity Wishart Reef' in her honour.

One particularly intrepid bearer of the Wishart name is the Scots-born maritime and polar adventurer and explorer **Jock Wishart**.

Born in 1951 and educated at Dumfries Academy and the University of Durham, where he was president of its boat club, in 2011 he led the maritime expedition The Old Putney Row to the Pole.

This was a 450 mile (724.2 km) row from Resolute Bay, Nanavut, in Canada, to the certified position of the Magnetic North Pole, west of Ellesmere Island, northern Canada.

Filmed for a BBC television documentary, the boat was named *Old Putney* after the project sponsor's brand of single malt whisky.

Previous to this, in 1998, aboard the powered vessel *Cable & Wireless Adventurer*, Wishart and his crew completed a 26,000-mile (approx. 41,843km) circumnavigation of the globe, encompassing fifteen ports in ten countries, in 74 days, 20 hours and 58 minutes.